AURA

WRITTEN WITH PASSION

VEDANYAA. M

ISBN 979-888503006-9

I thank each and every person who contributed their best to this book. It wouldn't be possible without the co-authors being so patient and cooperative. I'd like to dedicate this book to every person out there struggling with their thoughts or feelings. I also thank my mom and my sister for always being there for me, it wouldn't be possible without you two!

Contents

Contents

Acknowledgements

The completion of this book would not have been possible without the cooperation and support of the delightful writers. Their patience and efforts made together as a team. A big thank you to the publication for helping me out publish my second book.

Behind a mask- Vedanyaa. M

About the writer

She's the compiler of this book. She thinks writing is peaceful, it helps one to look within their own selves. She started writing poems and writeups when she was 13. She currently resides in Pune. She's studying in grade 11. She loves writing, reading and cooking. She wants to travel the world and explore. Feeling the rain and watching the sky full of stars and moon is her kinda thing.

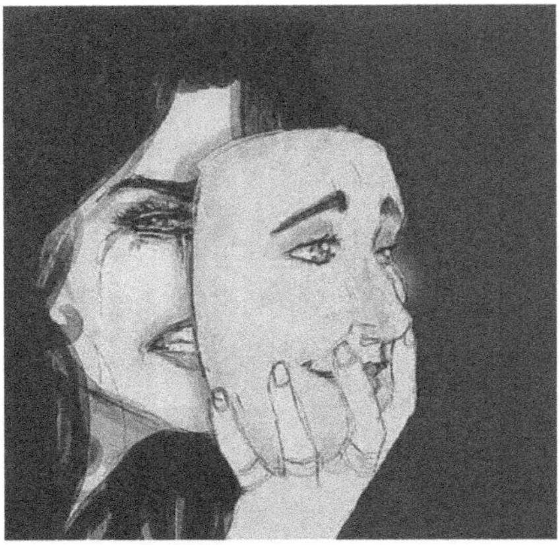

BEHIND A MASK

There's a face I see,
Behind a mask for which I plea.
The mask hasn't been there forever,
From what I think the face behind it is clever.

Dark sorrows, is it a thing?
For what the clever person had to plead.
There's a fear I see,
Behind a mask for which I plea.

The mask had to be worn,
Because the clever person had to be born.
There's a hope I see,
Behind a mask for which I plea.

Finding a ray was difficult,
For which the mask was an occult.
There's a story I see,
Behind a mask for which I plea.

- Vedanyaa

Men: a word misunderstood- Nitya Bhambhani

About the writer

She is Nitya Bhambhani, studying in 11th standard. She currently resides in Rajkot, Gujarat. She enjoys moonlight strolls on empty roads also has a strong belief in the universe and its magic. She prefers watching more sunsets than Netflix. She started writing as a dream of publishing my own book one day. Also, she is currently saying yes to new adventures.

Men- 'A word misunderstood'

Today the Sun shines bright,

With you standing with us, everything's alright!

First a son,

Then a student, Then a friend,

and life goes on.

Then you become a father, a guide,

Life takes you on a wild ride!

Then the grandfather who gets candy,

There are many roles you play,

and smile throughout the day.

When life gets hard, you become the family's rock,

You answer the door, even before we knock

There are times when everything falls apart,

You make things easy, lighten up the heart.

- Nitya Bhambhani

Ranjha- A love story

Distance is always shown as a symbol, which hed brings two lovers closer, but is it really so.

Maybe it is. It is a symphony of letters you're on lover sends you every week, just to let young.. know how badly they missed you.

Their eyes hold the essence of longings, and loneliness, ready to fall down with the tears, knitting poetry in the name of longings and as they say, intezaar.

Somewhere in the corner of the country, there's someone who has carved calligraphy of initial of a name, building a castle to live with this them, but not everyone gets away because of a heartbreak.

Sometimes it's the universe who keeps you away, maybe because you are born to shine

- Nitya Bhambhani

Reflection...- Kolaj Ghoshal

About the writer

Kolaj Ghoshal, a 17-year-old aspiring young writer who started her journey towards writing when she was 12 years old. Kolaj studied in the arms of the hill station, Kurseong, in early life to her high school. Being a mortal, she also went through a lot of mishaps but never gave up writing! Instead, she made it her strength and continued to give her all attention to the blank papers to fill them with her thoughts and experiences. Kolaj usually writes in a fairy tale style with a theme being realistic. She's been taking part in other anthologies and one day aspires to write her book. Which probably be happening soon.!

Reflection...

You see a goddess in me

Others, just some ordinary girl.

Others see the shells in me...

But you see the pearl...!

Others see the ashes in me...

Burnt and gone...

Whereas you see the ashes fly

Like a bird from dusk to dawn...

But do you see me in me?

Or it's still her perfection?

Do see me in your life...?

Or am I still just a reflection?..

- Kolaj

Phone call...

It didn't matter anymore...

Or maybe it did...

The hurt was written...

Maybe people couldn't read...

Lips said "okay-----

" Heart was wrecked.....

Voice sounded happy...

The eyes were drenched...

“distance is too much to take”

He said without acknowledgement.

Of the changes she made...

All for her beloved’s contentment.

Today the distance saved her...

From the feeling to be declared...

Today the phone call saved her...

From ripping apart in tears.

"Yeah absolutely!----" she agreed in a smile

To his "I can’t do it anymore, you can never be mine"

Lil did he know about it, she was all his...

It’s just she was broken enough to secret the grief with ease.

- Kolaj

Wheel of Aura- Zainab Saboowala

About the writer

Zainab Saboowala is a dreamer and believer from Mumbai. She's a night lover and works on being a good human rather than the great one. Her writings are her thoughts, emotions and feelings put into words. She believes when you can't say it, write it. She is optimistic and loves spreading smiles around.Penname - Zain;Instagram handle - @an.affectionate.dreamer

Wheel of Aura

Coloured emanation that encloses a body

From place or person, we perceive an energy

Our intuitions or conscience starts to speak

Vibes we get and emotions that we feel

Depending on situations, moods and life stories

Our aura keeps changing

Love, evil, fear, optimism, jealousy

The feeling of compatibility or positivity

Different colours for all emotions and qualities

Every energy around us keeps flowing

Glow radiating around our body

With colour depicting our personality

Energy centres of our body

That unites body, mind and spirit

Helps to balance our thoughts and growth

7 wheel has a name, the colour of its own

Stones and crystals associated with it

Are known to balance and organize the ruling energetic realms

Some are sceptical about it and some consider it as a mystical realm

While some develop spiritual connection and use in the process of manifesting

Life colour or aura that we see

Is because of our body's energy wheel.

- Zain

Maternal love: Mother's Last Call-Parth Arora

About the writer

PARTH ARORA, a class 12 medical student from Haryana. A featured poet in several esteemed magazines. Since kindergarten, he was obsessed with books, he started to pen his feelings when he was a class 7 student. He loves helping people, spreading positivity and putting smiles on people's faces. He looks at ordinary things in a new way and strives hard to make today better than yesterday!

MATERNAL LOVE- MOTHER'S LAST CALL

Remember the blissful day the child is born,

Celebrations, fondants and the clothes worn,

Recollect, the mom holding child in arms,

Gazing with love and protection from any harm.

Children grow up, bored and lethargic to go to school,

Excuses her about stomach ache and makes her a fool,

So caring and emotional, he takes care of his son,

Mother is tense but the child is a naughty one.

With time, he grows and learns,

But mom's love is steady and stern.

Studies, part-time job, always absorbed,

Mother yearn for a lovely time but the child is engrossed.

She unblinkingly stares at the door,

But child occupied with friends and much more,

Her eyes full of tears, child backs home,

She embraces her without any fears.

The child becomes a grown-up,

Still, mother's unconditional love rise.

He received a call but engaged couldn't pick up

Backs home and incapacitated watches the mom's corpse being picked up
{"unfortunately that was his mom's last call "}

- Parth Arora

Lost in the dead soul

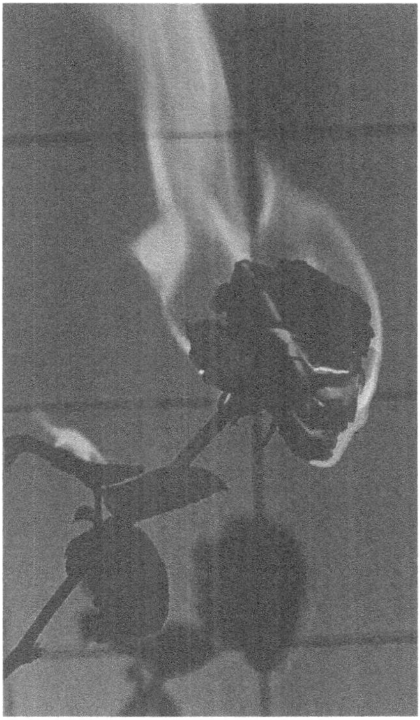

Foggy clouds of melancholy dawdled

Wolves growled, darkness overspread

Heavenly eyes remained unblinked

Loquacious mouth stood shut

Her gleaming body leaned quietly...

Clouded with the white burial garment

This silence was eternal, everlasting

I stood grief-stricken at the requiem prayer

Carrying the corpse

But the graveyard appeared miles apart

My sharp eyes could just spot sadness

My nose could only smell sorrow

And my mouth snarled for her

She was deceased.......I lost her !!!!

- Parth Arora

A Girl with a Violin

She was born as a beautiful girl,
dear to her dad, his priceless
pearl.

But what happened to her,
her glancing in the mirror,
the miraculous site of herself,

became a nightmare?

The girl with the violin,
was attacked with acid,
the effervescent spirit became placid.

She wanted to raise her voice,
but the bothering people left
with no choice.
Either to die or scream with no noise.

Shame on the guy,
who ruined her beauty,
left her on the road to cry,
her tears fell on the ground,
how bold was she!
Stood up smiling and sound.

Her painting stars doesn't let her down.
Burning body still no frown.
What was her fault??
Denying a man who just knew
how to assault?

- **Parth**Arora

Teen Feels- Rashida Makda

About the writer

Rashida Makda studying in class 11. She currently lives in Rajkot, Gujarat. She's a very proactive person. I like to learn new things and that's how she started writing and finally, She's able to that my dream of publishing a book is now a reality.

Teen Feels

Who decides what's right what's wrong? For some, I might be confident but for some, I might be over smart, for some, I might be full of flaws but for some, I might be flawsome. Try to approach me personally, agitation will surely overwhelm me, fearing rejection and criticism. The more I feel happy, the more I worry. Thinking I'm being evaluated, maybe I can't rely on my trust in anybody. Call me a nerd and wired but my situation is absurd. I'm stuck in a whole, and it's hard, can't say a fitting acceptable word. That would be agreeable for the world. Round bumps of red rash on my face small protrusion of skin were visible on my face, aftermath of fanatic consumption on chocolates. Do you say you've gained weight? That you want to lose it too? Well, I wish I could be like you. A slimmer size, a better look, a cooler smile. But I'm stuck in this body, trapped beyond belief. Stuck with this feeling none of them began with relief. Though I have many insecurities. But just because I'm a teenager I'm not irresponsible, I don't break every single rule, I don't mean I'm moody and rude, it's doesn't mean I only think about myself. It doesn't mean I'm lazy and unorganised and it doesn't mean I'm addicted to my phone.

Here's the thing I wish I knew sooner to get past the pain, for it hurts more than you hold it in. Tears aren't a sign of weakness but of the courage to keep going besides its is a great way to detox and to give yourself a chance to begin again. Get to know me for who I'm not for who I'm labelled. Only if we encourage each other to share our feelings we'd create a world of no judgment. For beverages are meant to be bottled up, not human feelings.

- Rashida Makda

Memories- Kashish Agarwal

ABOUT THE WRITER

She is a 12th standard passed PCM student who aims at cracking the CSE examinations. Writing isn't just her passion but it's a means of pouring her emotions into words. The emotions remained unspoken, unsaid and unexpressed. She cries not with tears but with her words. She's been a part of the iimun and has won various prizes in olympiads, poetry dramatization competitions etc. on a school level and national level as well. She's been selected as the vice-captain and then the captain by the school. An optimistic soul, a conversationalist and envisaging hope is the quintessence of her life. She has a keen interest in computers, mathematics, technology and aptitude. She believes to change the world through the sword of her words.

Memories

Memories, fills the voids of our minds with ecstasy,

And aids our souls just like the drugs sold by a pharmacy.

Flashing upon our encephalon when we are miles away,

Impelling us to cry a bit by retaining all those moments we cherished someday.

Sometimes tormenting and sometimes exuberating,

These mixed packages of memories succour our brains and hearts to be more communicating.

Not discerning the worth of the moments we relish at those extant hours,

And then days after, the urge to return to those jovial times by some superpowers.

Memories don't always give the pain to break our sloppy hearts,

Sometimes, they enrapture our souls with some sort of magical art.

Without memories, our lives would be but a writer without pain,

Ironically, they are the reason to live the rarest bits of our lives forever again.

- Kashish Agarwal

Beauty of era- Sohini Ghosh

About the writer

Her name is Sohini Ghosh. She's from the city of joy Kolkata. She's 17 years old. She's a writer by passion and loves to play with her words. She's the founder of a writing community words of heart and Co-founder of writers amulet. She's a motivator, dancer, singer too. She's studying in the 12th class.

The Beauty of era

The beauty is in your own skin,

Such beauty in her soft milky white skin,

And black denotes the beauty of your flawless and soothing skin,

Though, the heart was hurt with the memories of the past,

But from now the beauty of this era will blast,

Your skin is the incredible and creative unique artistic expression that exists.

But you aren't weak anymore you're strong and bold.

Beauty is within your immortal words,

Beauty is within your soulful heart,

Beauty exists in the grammar of your literature,

Beauty exists in the phrases of your life,

It shines when you struggle and strife,

Your inner heart is a long-lasting impact on beauty,

Which covers up honesty and purity,

The most elegant of all with no naked lies,

You're here in the lap of the world just to move on and fly.

Beauty exists in your scars,

Which makes you so strong,

Which helps you rectify the right and wrong

Empowerment and happiness are the characteristics you hold,

To love yourself more and shine like gold.

Your hard-working and dedicating hand,

Defines the sacrifice behind this beauty.

- Sohini Ghosh

Fun never goes from you

With support, with faith

And you shower me with care.

A sweet and sincere message

In your every biting stare.

Bring me up, when I fall and

Like a breeze, you sail me through.

Beat me down, when I fail,

Like a teacher, you scold me too.

With a friend like you,

I know what friendship is

And for the bond we share, I swear,

Our fun flow will never cease.

- Sohini Ghosh

Ineffable personality- Priya Singh

About the writer

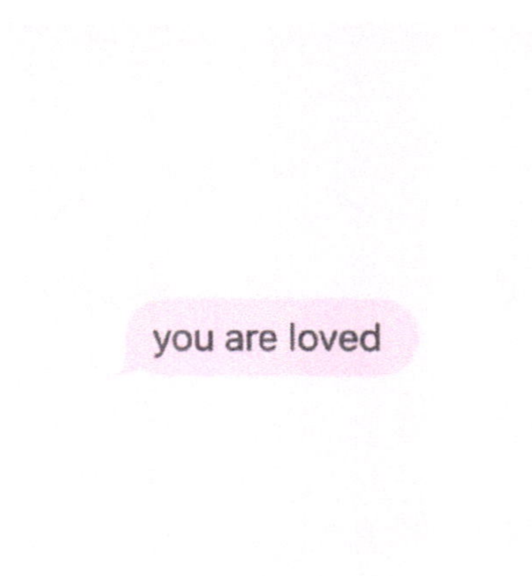

Priya Singh is born & brought up in Dewas, Madhya Pradesh.Proud daughter of her father B.N.Singh (TI). She's completed Masters of Computer Science. She is a Former Educationist, communication Trainer. She's the Co-Author of the Anthologies:- "It's all about two-phase: love & hate", "Words From Heart", "Fierce, Fearless N Flawed" & "In the way of a borehole". All are available on Amazon. Till today, She's worked in 100+ Anthologies as a Co-Author. Her writing keeps her at ease. She mostly writes quotes on thoughts. She loves inspiring young minds. Instagram id- instant__thoughts_

Ineffable personality

Something speaks louder than words,

it comes before you visit,

Whenever your name comes,

it's just a thing that could hover around us

& do pander in figuring out what kinda stuffs

you keep within as a human,

are you a person to hold

or to let go is the only thing

that comes in a row,

never avoid going with it,

you never know what Kinda soul you visit or work with,

it speaks all, thinking could lead us to saunter & stroll,

it's just a soothing breeze

or a wild wave that could flow while touching you

& your senses recognise everything pure & whole.

- Priya Singh

Aura

A- It could be auspicious or bad omen energy.

U- always talk about the person could be You.

R- Spiritual Remedy to all physical problems

A- August like anything

Your senses by which you got to know about the person before his upcoming

It tells everything without uttering,

Kinda energy goes everywhere,

It reveals all hides nothing at all,

Energy has its own language to communicate,

Aura is something that either protects you from bad omen

or reveal you is the bad one.

Whether you believe in it or not It always works,

keep your Aura as this is nothing bad

could ever dare to come close to us.

-Priya Singh

The Walk- Shreya Ambastha

About the writer

This is Shreya Ambastha, a First-year student, pursuing B.Tech in the Mechanical engineering branch, from MIT-WPU Pune... She hails from a small town named Daltonganj, located in Jharkhand. Deeply interested in unfolding mysteries of life, love, the universe and every lil thing we deal with. She is flesh and bones covered from head to toe, trying to live every single second, before she withers one day. And penning down words in the form of poetry is her way to keep the spirit alive inside her soul. She wishes that you all have a great time enjoying the Aura. And she hopes to cross paths with anyone reading this one day. Thank you.

The Walk

How come I never knew that just a walk with you would do it all,

would give me immense pleasure.

I was satisfied.

As we walked up to the horizon together.

We saw the beauty in everything we passed by, your presence made them more adorable.

The lil things you did, like holding my hands, citing our love in words, catching glimpses of mine,

all those mattered.

I rolled down my eyes, took a sight of Our steps, harmonized in perfect rhythm.

I asked you if you wanted some rest, but you denied; you raised your eyebrows, and I said, "Me neither!"..

We kept walking, listening to each other's talk.

Until the day turned dusky;

At that moment we were so in love,

I remember, even in the midst of tears, we were so happy..

It was a beautiful end to our long walk.

- Shreya Ambastha

Saccharine Summer- Niyati Shinde

About the writer

Student in grade 12th Wattpad author

Saccharine Summer

Summer breeze flew past my cheeks,

Winding the cuts that I had cut deep.

Walking down the lane,

I bought ice cream,

Reviving my sore throat from last night's screams.

I waved at some kids wearing the swimming gear,

The pain of the twisted wrist was just enough to bare.

I turned back home,

Where devils faked to care.

-Niyati Shinde

Nacreous Needs

All my hopes drowned,

When my boss looked at me and frowned,

He's not my master,

More like a drunken disaster,

What can I say? What can I do?

I need money; only for you honey,

There's a business party tonight but I said it's a professional meeting..

I'm wearing a blue floral dress,

But a black bodycon one beneath,

I felt like not going,

I came to you; running...

But I saw you smoking...

It was slipping from my eyes; my tears.

- Niyati Shinde

Live with a greater vision- Durga Balamadhavan

About the writer

Durga Balamadhavan is a self-constructed writer & is a 17 years old girl who has a kindling fire to achieve. She's a co-author of 40+ anthologies 3 world record anthologies to date & compiling her ongoing anthologies " The next billionaire" & "The Thirst to Travel". You can DM her on insta page @quotescumarts to get success & love quotes, poetry at a reasonable charge. Her silent partners are Books & Nature. She loves Travelling & exploring the world.

Live with a greater vision

If you possess a habit of embracing positivity amidst negativities,

then you don't wanna bother about life's uncertainties.

You may face life with tragedy In those circumstances,

just stay positive & try to accept the reality.

Even if the world discourages your strength,

have the courage to prove them wrong.

Your words of positivity are the only way to kindle your inner fire;

which will never let you tired.

Sometimes, you may get doomed of failing over & over again.

I know how much it pains

But learning lessons from those pains seeking everyday gain.

Practise daily & become well-trained.

Spread positivity to the people & creatures around you as much as possible.

Never ever bother about the risks & troubles.

Set your benchmark remarkable.

If you keep on heading towards your dreams,

you'll be able to seek results that can be phenomenal.

What you dream, you become the same.

So, always dream High & never let down that flame.

Always possesses an attitude of positivity

that enriches your level of creativity.

Never seek motivation from outside.

It's all lies inside.

Double your willpower & dare enough to take risks

and break your bigger goals into smaller tasks.

Reward yourself for completing little works.

Just go with the flow & never be too much stressed.

Live your life as you wish to live with a bigger vision

and be the best in making decisions.

- uniquedreamerdurga

Life is on- Kawaljeet Singh

About the writer

Kawaljeet Singh, living in Delhi Pursuing graduation in Bcom, He is recently working with various anthologies He is passionate about writing.

Life is on

Life goes on and on

Sometimes you lose or sometimes you won

Life goes on and on

Someone is dead or someone is born

Life goes on and on

Somewhere we stay and somewhere we gone

Life goes on and on...

-Kawaljeet Singh

Just for you- Swayamshree Chakravarty

Co-author Swayamshree is a 12th science student from Odisha. She's a trained dancer and a guitarist, and now also a writer! She has been a part of 30+ anthologies. Her writings are based on her past. Hope you all love her write-ups.

Just for you

It's true that I can't sing

But it was also true

I could have sung for you…

True that I can't wait

But oh my love

I could have waited for you...

If nothing could have gone right

And I just had you

It would have been enough for me

To hold onto you,

And shower my love on you...

I guess I did too much

From my side

That's why today

You're no more besides...

It would have been

A heaven on earth If my heart's desire

Were fulfilled But nevermind,

Maybe not today, but surely

Waiting for you

Just for you ...

- Swayamshree Chakravarty

My four legged brother

Someone asked me If I have a brother

I smiled and replied

Yeah, but he's from another mother

They laughed and asked again

If he was not my sibling

I nodded and said

Yes, I adopted him...ping

Looking at their shocking faces

I finally opened the secret

That I had a four-legged brother

A dog, to be honest

I explained how my brother

Acts as a mood changer to me

I can instantly glow up

On seeing him, beside me!

He is such a little cutie pie

Cuteness overloaded

Such a playful child he is

A beauty on earth's head

I just love everything

Everything about him

I can tear up immediately

On the thought of me leaving him.

- **Swayamshree Chakravarty**

SHE- Srija Sadhukhan

About the writer

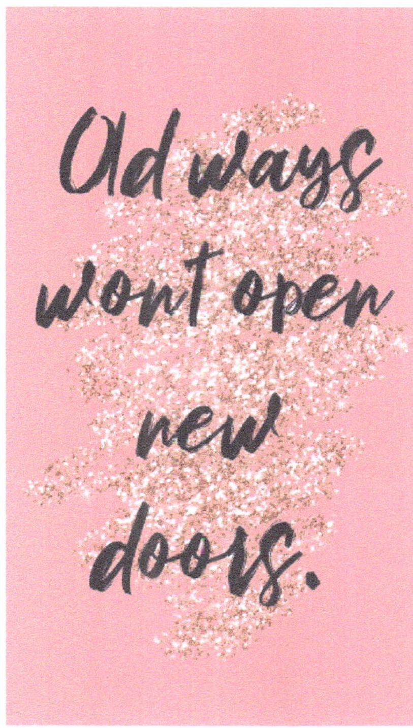

Srija Sadhukhan is 19 years old girl studying BSc Biotechnology at Amity University Kolkata. Loves to write poetry and a book worm too

SHE

The monthly ‘bloody’ pain,

The insult of that stain.

Yes, she is a woman.

That stain is not for hiding.

She is judged by society,

She means the burden of marriage,

Not to fly up in the sky

'Coz night are not safe for 'her'.

She feels insecure and worried,

She can take all pain with a smile

Yes, she is a woman.

A woman of pride and strength.

- Srija Sadhukhan

Something waiting still...

So many desires,

At the tip of the tongue

Still waiting to -

Come out at once.

So many laughs,

Smiles and wishes

Still waiting -

For years to come.

So much pain,

Anger and ire,

Still wanting -

With disguise.

-**Srija Sadhukhan**

Sun kisses- Arya Muraleedharan

About the writer

She is a budding psychologist, young heart in photography and pioneer writer from the motherland of Kathakali in god's own country. She tries to live as an atheist and feminist through her words, deeds and writings.

Sun kisses

The sun kisses in the dawn

Are the excellent means

To wake up from the bed.

The tenderness of the sun,

The bright flash,

And the freshness

Brings a promising day.

Sunshine through the windows

Prompt you to awake.

You may sit on the mattress

Kisses on my forehead

And say morning greetings.

- Arya Muraleedharan

To my love

I'm addicted to your blush

When it changes to lush.

The passion on your brown eyes

Where your dream never dies.

The beat of your heart

Inevitably became a part.

The smile on your lips,

Remind me of the tulips.

-Arya Muraleedharan

We all lost ourselves- Mrunmayee Pawar

About the writer

Mrunmayee Pawar is 15 and just passed out of 10th. She likes making new friends, exploring new adventurous places, gaining new experiences, chocolates, reading, writing, graphic designing, swimming, playing chess, spending time with friends and family. She dislikes rude and judgemental people, violence, bullying, insects, ghosts and people who unnecessarily spread hate.

We all lost ourselves

We all lost ourselves to the corruption still going around the world in the midst of this dangerous pandemic.

We all lost ourselves to the virtual world in name of studies, work, classes, school and many more making us lose contact with the outer world.

It said that every small thing of our life teaches us something, similarly, this pandemic helped us know the importance of our loving relationship with our family and friends.

We all lost ourselves in our hobbies like reading, writing, drawing and many more things that we have an interest in.

It's said that the sum of evil and good is balanced in the world but then why did so many innocents lose their lives causing the sum of evil to rise, so yes we can say that we all lost ourselves to evil.

But we won't give up and keep fighting against it because in the end good will always win, which means we will definitely win.

We all lost ourselves in the beauty of nature which we never bothered to observe and only kept harming it causing it to take its revenge on the whole human race.

But everyone deserves a second chance, so if we survive this pandemic then we will definitely learn a good lesson of not harming mother nature.

-Mrunmayee Pawar

A sunrise of hope

When the beautiful rays of the sun make their way out of the dark night,

it brings a new ray of hope and the start of a fresh new day with itself.

So forget the regrets and sadness of the past and move ahead,

this is the message the sun rays give when they fall on the earth.

During beautiful dawn,

birds chirp lightly,

trees dance happily and gentle air spreads an amazing fragrance and aroma of beautiful flowers

making the atmosphere happy and joyful.

It is said that when your life is submerged in darkness,

then a light or a ray of hope will make its way

and bring you out of the black darkness,

this is another message the sun rays give us.

- **Mrunmayee Pawar**

Inevitable- Rebecca Ramhuoltling Hmar

About the writer

Rebecca Ramhuoltling Hmar is a Psychology student, currently pursuing an MSc in Psychology from the Central University of Karnataka. She preferred and engaged in writing cause her mind is unstoppable when she starts to write and she can let out all that is within through this medium. By grace, through faith, she beliefs in all things love empathy, compassion and acceptance.

Inevitable

You and I

Just same species

But think and feel different,

in the same situation.

You and I

Might have or get,

the same opportunity to avail

But might not have the same success story.

You and I

Might have the biggest of dreams

But the level of achievement might differ

Cause the effort put in might not be equal.

You and I

Might not get all that we wished for

But that doesn't mean,

to stop being grateful for little things.

You and I

Might have everything in life

But that doesn't mean,

we stop thriving.

Be driven

Be grateful for who you are,

and all that you have.

Amen.

- Rebecca Ramhuoltling Hmar

Out of love

She did what not?

for those she loved

There were days...

she didn't take a moment,

to bring a smile so that they wear it,

out of joy, happiness and satisfaction.

But it went like...

After so much of

insults, possessiveness, discouragement, selfishness

She had to pause

Think for long

Where does she stand?

What does she deserve?

What she can do?

Who does she deserve?

and who deserves her?

These thoughts...

not only made her,

know her worth,

but value every little step taken

and made every day,

every decision and

opportunity count.

She looked and stuck for,

what could mould her

in the best possible ways.

She knew

She is precious!

- Rebecca Ramhuoltling Hmar

Downfall- Yukta Nawani

About the writer

Yukta Nawani is all time learner, an artist by passion and a lawyer by profession. A CS aspirant. A fun-loving, happy soul who loves to play with words. she is twenty and lives in the city of Raipur. she believes in enjoying every single moment of her life with zeal and pride. looking for new possibilities.

Downfall

People say,

Life is a rollercoaster,

With ups and downs.

They say,

Everyone will treat you nice,

Found Aura in you,

Every time you achieve a dream.

They say,

Once your downfall starts,

We leave,

And find someone better.

They didn't say anything,

About the comeback,

And it's stories.

But now I say,

To the downfall,

It's amazing and grateful,

Experiencing you because

You lead me to a path worth remembering.

- **Yukta Nawani**

My wish- Dr. Kanu Tiwari

About the writer

Dr Kanu Tiwari is a doctor by profession and a writer and baker by heart. She has participated in 30+ anthologies, published a solo book and has even compiled. She has headed the literary department in her college and has been nominated for various literary awards. She wishes to serve the nation by her profession and change the ideology with her words. Her most prized possessions are her smile, stethoscope and a pen.

My wish

The day since I opened my eyes

I couldn't say to you any more lies

Even when the world gets cold,

Your love never gets old.

If you wish upon a star;

You will know how we got this far!

The one soulmate,

I cannot ever hate!

Your heart is of pure gold;

that is mine forever to hold

Near and dear, You are always there

The magic of your eyes;

gives wings to my sorrows and it flies,

The warmth of your smile;

Gets me going on and on for miles

I wish I may, I wish I might;

Have the wish I wish tonight

Wishes to be home;

Where I'll never be alone

Be with you,

And watch the beautiful view

Of how life will unfold

Before the days become old!

You'll forever be my shooting star;

The one who guides us from far

On and on I'll go with the flow,

To be with you;

I'll even bow

I'll still hold you as my treasure,

With time; that will be my leisure

- Dr Kanu Tiwari

Gain

That day; one of a kind,

I played my memories on rewind,

A memory came by,

Well; I don't know why,

A memory I regard,

And with all my heart

I guard, The day I gained

And my life changed

I was seated in a car

And I watched from afar

Someone helping a small boy

Giving some necessities and toys

I made a plan in my mind

And yes, like-minded people did a find,

helping with NGOs was their plan,

With all their heart as much as they can

And I decided to have a role,

And make the world a better place was my goal,

I helped train kids with sewing

And helped my mother with all the kitchen and brewing,

That was the day I truly gained.

-Dr Kanu Tiwari

Procastination- Tripti Pandey

About the writer

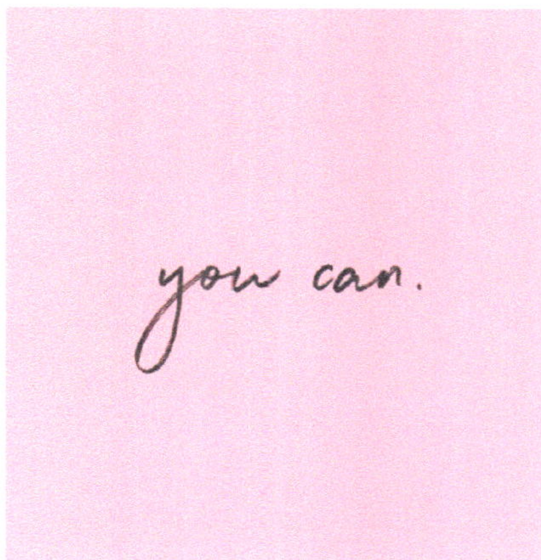

Tripti Pandey, born and brought up in the Bhadohi district of Uttar Pradesh. Her birthday is on 30th August 2001, to the father Virendra Kumar Pandey and mother Madhu Pandey. Right now She is neet aspirant with an intermediate Bachelorette degree 2020 (science stream) from Small Wonders sr. sec. School Jabalpur. She started writing when she was in class 11th since then she is penning down her emotions and deep thought and eventually her goal is to bring a change through her writings

Procrastination

To deal with procrastination you need to be mentally strong,

you have to fight with your comfort zone but with patience and it takes 21 days to adopt something but you have to be consistent.

And procrastinating is not a good thing cause it somewhere suppresses you,

it may create problems in doing more and working on self-growth.

In this jet age, you have to be punctual,

then only you will get what you want.

Take a deep breath and start working.

The main thing you can do to deal with procrastination is "to start",

so get ready to fight with your comfort zone.

- **Tripti Pandey**

Try to listen to your moral voice

Everyone should do something great and unique in their life.

The things which satisfy your inner soul is the only thing that means you did something great and unique.

If you find anything wrong even 0.99% remember that it's an indication from your soul which is indicating you to think again because we can be wrong but our soul not,

it's the part of our inner-moral voice that only can indicate us not correct it.

If we start doing things that don't give satisfaction then it will be useless,

unsustainable, and can harm.

So think once while doing anything,

if it relates to cheap or invaluable things.

The things which gratify one's soul are honesty, positivity,

accommodation, faith, learning from mistakes, sustainable development, sacrifice, focus,

and all the great things which everyone doesn't have,

so, friends, whosoever want to be praised by others start doing things which gratify you.

- Tripti Pandey

Toast with memories- Urvashi

About the writer

Urvashi (Phoenixxx) grew up in New Delhi, India turned M.T. Initially focusing on performing arts, and life. From her childhood, she shows interest in writing and began writing short stories, poems and motivational quotes and many other writings. She is an explorer who loves to explore the world in her style. Worked in many companies with different field backgrounds and become the Phoenixxx in today's writer's world. "Go on your path, even if you live for a day." "Never give up on a dream that you've been chasing almost your whole life..." "Even if I'm a little hurt it's okay." "

If you can't fly, then run. Today we will survive. If you can't run, then walk." A fighter never stops...

Toast with memories

It's the people we've met

I wish you were here but you are not

'Cause all memories come back' we've been through everything

More toast for those here today

Toast the people we lost along the way

'Cause all memories come back

And bring back memories, memories bring you back

There comes a time when I remember when I didn't know the pain

When I believed forever, and everything would be the same

Now my heart feels like December when someone takes your name

'Cause I can't reach to call you, but I know I will one day,

Yes' everybody Hurts sometimes but everything will be fine

Go and raise a glass and say,

It's the people we've met

I wish you were here but you are not

'Cause all memories come back'

There comes a time

I remember I never felt so lost

When I thought it was too powerful to stop all the hate

Now my heart feels like an ember and it's lighting up the darkness

I'll carry these torches for you that you know

I'll never drop, yeah everybody Hurts sometimes

Everyone gets hurt someday,

I wish you were here but you are not

All we've been through

More toast to the people here today

Toast the people we lost along the way

'Cause our life is drowned in the river of memories

And bring back memories, memories bring you back.

- Urvashi (Phoenixxx)

Love mashup

Sometimes anger comes on your laughter.

Sometimes where the heart wants to laugh.

Sometimes hide the sorrow in some corner of the heart.

Sometimes I want to tell everything to someone.

Never cry, even when there is a million sorrow.

And sometimes the heart just wants to shed tears.

Sometimes it feels good to roam free,

but sometimes the heart wants to be confined in someone's arms.

Sometimes think of something new in life.

And sometimes the heart just wants to live like this.

Sometimes in my thoughts I always think about you,

But when came to existence found out the absence of you beside me.

Sometimes felt around you,

but sometimes want to see you at a glance.

My all love is about you, for you, to you

But sometimes I felt thousands of miles always from you.

- Urvashi (Phoenixxx)

Appreciation

Thank you all who have been here till the end, I am very grateful for having complete the second book. Thank you to all the co-authors for being calm and amazing through the journey, it's been wonderful. Lastly, I thank my mother who has always believed in me when no one did, and has always had my back!

The book'AURA' will always have a vibe where every person can connect. It will always have a good quality surrounded by my heart.